When LOVE is a "New Beginning"...

A Handbook To Remembering What We Should Never Forget

Gwen Editin

AuthorHouse™
1663 Liberty Drive
Bloomington, IN 47403
www.authorhouse.com
Phone: 1-800-839-8640

© 2010 Gwen Editin. All rights reserved.

No part of this book may be reproduced, stored in a retrieval system, or transmitted by any means without the written permission of the author.

First published by AuthorHouse   12/13/2010

ISBN: 978-1-4520-8763-4 (hc)
ISBN: 978-1-4520-8764-1 (sc)
ISBN: 978-1-4520-8765-8 (e)

Library of Congress Control Number: 2010915701

Printed in the United States of America

This book is printed on acid-free paper.

Certain stock imagery © Thinkstock.

Because of the dynamic nature of the Internet, any Web addresses or links contained in this book may have changed since publication and may no longer be valid. The views expressed in this work are solely those of the author and do not necessarily reflect the views of the publisher, and the publisher hereby disclaims any responsibility for them.

WHEN

LOVE

is a

"New Beginning"...

a handbook to remembering
what we should never forget.

by Gwen Editin

to anyone
who accepts the challenge
of maintaining a love relationship
while balancing the routine of everyday life -
may you survive the journey of a lifetime
and if not...
this book was written so we can all remember
the passion that accompanies
"New Beginnings."

Contents

"Today, Tomorrow and Forever" 1
what must I do 2
you should have told me..3
I'm afraid...4
I didn't know...5
how could I 7
I remember..8
I should really..9
I plan to be there..10
I thought that you knew...11
nobody told me...12
you were perfect for me 13
if God 14
perhaps, if I tell you...15
if you could 16
just as sure...17
without hearts we do not feel 19
of course...20
the closer and nearer...21
I know...22
separated now, by time 23
L O V E has a way of healing all wounds. 25
you are my rock...26
you couldn't know...27
IF I could have held you 29
AFTER.. 30
I want to hold you...31
I tried to find...32
if there is 33
the things you did stole my heart 35
it keeps my heart 36
just what I feel...37
it makes no sense...38
for every soul there is a place 39

if you want more 40
how did you know 41
I knew you were special 42
I close my eyes 43
a lifetime partner **45**
but more likely, a dog 46
I want to 47
I need you 48
from the words 49
how don't you know 50
you will always 51
Meeting Men Elsewhere **53**
what if 54
how should I 55
it's the way 56
One Night before the Big Ceremony **57**
of all the things 58
if anyone asked 60
far beyond 61
more to me 62
I think it went 63
"it's when I lie awake at night " **65**
loving you always 66
if I let myself 67
what if 68
when you said you "weren't perfect" **69**
hearts don't need 70
something about you 71
when my love 72
Looking to the Future **73**
I can't deny 74
it doesn't happen 75
I'll keep you 76
I can feel 77
Cathie and David **79**
I don't want to 81
I reach 82

no one has 83
when I'm not sure 84
if you take 85
perhaps it isn't the act of loving **87**
today 88
why can't I 89
I don't want to know 90
meeting men in the supermarket **91**
so alone 92
wandering the earth 93
love is 95
when you stood 96
just like always **97**
if you need 98
if you tell me 99
and then comes "forever" **101**
I hope 103
how can 104
I know a love 105
I want to 106
I want you 107
A **110**
if 111
if I lie here 112
safe in my heart 113
it's not always 114
The abc's of a healthy relationship: **115**
Signs there may be trouble ahead: **116**
the love I have 117
if I could 118
did you think 119
if I try 120
this book is dedicated to the memory of my mother **121**
"INDEPENDENCE DAY" **122**
E P I L O G U E **124**
AFTER THAT **125**
I can't forget 126

just one lifetime..127
I can only 128
the grey-haired woman **129**
F I N A L T H O U G H T S.. **130**
what a gift 131
Acknowledgements **132**
W I S H I N G YOU B E A U T Y **133**
Remembering today, tomorrow and always... 134
A place to record your own experiences with love – 135
love / life experiences continued... 136
other examples to be remembered: 137

"Today, Tomorrow and Forever"

"Today, tomorrow and forever" - words from the wedding vows they had just witnessed. Some day, she hoped to reply to his question with a simple "I do". Was it "always" or "forever" that is longer? He had given her the most wonderful hug last night. She hoped he had felt her response. But perhaps he was just relieved.

She had known by the look on his face that he had come to say "goodbye" and that he was leaving that night. Soon they would again be living separate lives, with no guarantee when their paths might cross.

Without him by her side, suddenly she felt so alone.

When he had looked her way, his eyes were both sad and distant. Haunted, really. She closed her eyes to remember how gently he had taken her hand and squeezed it. That gesture was one she wanted to re-live again and again.

Last night she was awakened by the sound of blinds flapping on the open window. It was then she realized that she had fallen in love.

With what? she asked herself. Or better yet, with whom?

Yet somehow that simple caress of her hand felt so right. When his arms had tightened around her, she felt she couldn't breathe.

She resolved that the next time, she would try harder to discover his secrets. Something felt different, now that she had decided to follow her heart. How long must she wait?

Whatever the outcome, she knew she would hold the memory of his touch, in her heart forever.

what must I do

what must I do, to make you mine
what more can I say
if given time
if I leave it to God, to bring you to me
what can I say
to make Him see
all that I dream, I dream for two
and only if I, could be given to you
if you remember, what it was
I want to say, that I felt your love
makes its own way, into my heart
and now that you're here, you're always a part
of what I think, and say or do
when I dream of love, it's always you
you're all, of what I needed
you changed me somehow, and
I don't want to be "without"
but why or who I am
to somehow be a part of you
that's all I really can
say, to all the love you brought
and the way you took my hand.

you should have told me

you should have told me
you'd steal my heart
and if I had known, you'd take that part
of me – to go with you
wherever you might be
then, I could follow you
to be there, if you need
so if you know, just what I feel
I know not so, myself
I should have run the other way
now that you're gone, I cannot say
I cannot speak, without the words
the heart you stole, holds all the hurt
when someone loves, the way I did
you need to find a way to fix
a broken heart or what is left
are all the things, she can't forget
the hand she held, the smile you took
a shoulder shrug, the way you looked
the heart she needs, to take back from
the man she thought, would be "the one"
to feel and hear the things you knew
I wanted more, if our love grew
but more than that, she can't forget
that other love she wanted then
be mine, or yours – forevermore
it's really just the same
I knew my heart would leave me
when first you called my name.

I'm afraid

I'm afraid, to let you love me
because I think, that I will find
with all of my whole being
you'll become, my way of life
something was so different
and there, right from the start
I should have stopped to listen
to what, was in my heart
now I can't 'want', without you to see
now I can't think, unless I believe
how else can I, explain to you
I know not, what I should feel
"not enough" time left to give
you, everything you need
"not enough" time to share everything
that we are meant to share
not enough ways, to show you my love
there's too many ways, I care
of all the things, I've never done
my loving you
was not one of them
when you held my hand, and then let go
I didn't know then
what I've come to know
but I do want to tell you
if things ever change
whether you leave me – my love still remains.

I didn't know

I didn't know, just what it was
now all I want – my other half
I wait for now, and ever more
however long, it takes before
'til I can come, and call you my own
when I can run, to my only home
again, like before when you went away
and all I could do then, was count the days
I love you, I need you
I want you for me
did I ever tell you, I don't want to be free
when all I want, is more than what
we have so far, I even thought
if only, you could read my mind
I 'll not make the same mistake, this time
I never felt, before you came
the way true love, can make its claim
this time, I know what I should do
I can tell you my plan
to love you forever
perhaps next time, I can show you how I
plan to love you
for the rest of my life.

how could I

forget

the memories

that you left

I remember

how could I forget
the memories I have left
the loving in your eyes
the way you made me smile
the way you touched my hand
I loved you now, and then
you'll always be the one
whose arms where I belong
the kindness of your heart
I loved right from the start
the way you came to sit with me
the words you whispered made me see
how sweet your soul
I only wish
that we had dared to try a kiss
and of all the gentle love, we shared
I 'd have it all now
if I had only dared
to bring you closer
where I believe
I would have found
you were all, that I need.

I should really

I should really tell you
what I believe
but I'm waiting for you
to come and tell me
if only you knew, just what it was
you might even come
and tell me you love
that way I would know
all that I feel
I won't have that fear
that it can't be real
I woke up to tell you
what I believe
when I didn't find
where you had been
I looked for your face
I wanted your hand
but I didn't see
where you had gone
I needed to know
that you still cared
I wanted to find
if my dream was still here.

I plan to be there

I plan to be there
whatever you need
I want you to know, that now I believe
in love that will never
come to an end
the love that began
when we became friends
how did it happen, that you and I
both fell in love
at the same time
it might have been
when I looked up to see
the way that your eyes
were looking at me
perhaps it occurred
when you opened your heart
the way that you treated me
right from the start
but I know what I felt
and it felt like more
than anything else
that I've felt before.

I thought that you knew

I thought that you knew
before you had left
you are the one
that I'll never forget
so sure was I, that I gave you my heart
now that you're gone
I'll just have to start
from the beginning
when you first came
I thought you should know, I'm not the same
before, when I woke
I had nothing to find
now I keep looking for
what I thought, was mine
I woke up this morning, to say that I want
finding instead, that you were gone
of all the words, I wanted to say
things that I meant, the other day
I wanted to show you again
how to love
how caring for "one"
is not enough
I thought that "best friends"
meant that we'd trust
that what we felt, might have become love.

nobody told me

nobody told me
that love could be
something that holds you
or sets you free
no longer free, to look around
all that I want, already found
if only you knew, to look over my way
I'd want you to hold me
in the same way
that love is holding me
still, as right now
the prisoner I am, I don't know how...
but whether or not I want to be free
perhaps it is better, that I just be
captured by love
that my own heart
feels only for you
now that it's started
it doesn't end, but goes on and on
having a mind
and a heart
of its own.

you

were perfect for me

in every way

except for the fact

that you couldn't stay...

if God

if God would let me have this time
to find more ways
to make you mine
I'd let you be, the man you are
I'd be close to you, but never too far
but
how can I learn, when to let go
these are the things
I need to know
I want to make sure, she's the right one
to love and to keep you, safe from all harm
I need to know
she'll love only you
and that some day
she'll bring you to
where we were headed
before she came along
back in the days
when we belonged
I need to remember, before I forget
how my heart felt
the day that you left.

perhaps, if I tell you

perhaps, if I tell you
what you mean to me
then we could be, all we should be
but unless it's already
entered your heart
I can't tell you my love
but only a part
the part where I say, I'll always be waiting
I need to be sure, first
how long, it's staying
and until then, it's not that easy
I need to plan, a new beginning
another way
to win your heart
a different love
right from the start
I'd find your hand, to put into mine
I'd take you with me, so we'd have more time
if stolen moments
were enough for me
perhaps I could say, I would never need
but how long was it meant
that I'd be alone
how far away, is the heart for my home
I need to know, if you're looking for love
those stolen moments, just not enough.

if you could

if you could let me love you
then
I promise to "'always, forever"
and
if you need a "more than just" friend
I promise to be that, as well
in the end
it's too late to worry, about what to do
my heart is already, on its way to you
and for "forever," it wants to belong
to the one where you are
that it calls its home
if you were to tell me
that you don't need
the same way, I want to
find you need me
then I could go and leave you behind
gone are the days
when my heart was mine
you were perfect for me
in every way
except for the fact
that you couldn't stay.

just as sure

just as sure as I can be
of anything that I know
I had a feeling, that you'd say
you really have to go
I meant to share the sun with you
the moon, the stars and then
the everything you wanted
but you'd have to say just when...
I meant to tell you, how I feel
I wanted you to know
I wanted everything for you
before you had to go
it really was naive of me, to think that you would stay
I didn't really know the words -
the ones I had to say
I shouldn't have to tell you, I think you know already
that what we had was something rare
I guess you just weren't ready
it started when you reached for my hand
then I became, a one-woman man
but I 'm not quite sure, how long I can wait
when this heart of mine, says it's too late
no longer free to pick and choose, it's something that you've done
or is it just, that sometimes - we can't pick the ones we love.

without hearts

we do not feel

without love

we cannot live

of course

of course I remember
how could I forget
all of the words
I thought you had said
deep in my heart
it's strange to say
but somehow, I knew
I would see you again
if not before, but maybe then
you'll come to know
and understand
if God gave you to me

I'd look after your soul
protect you from evil
and let you know
what it is like, to be truly loved
I have no doubt
you've been sent from above
you made me forget, all that I am
I just want to be close
as close as I can.

the closer and nearer

the closer and nearer
to you, I can be
everything and all
that you are to me
the way that I care
cannot be told
by words alone
not even close
it comes from somewhere
deeper within
your soul to mine
that's how it begins
and if it ends, with what we know
could only be said, to be a love grown
it seeks no more, it chooses not
it comes and it goes
and it can't be bought
I trust in the Lord
to help me through
all of these feelings
I have for you
but how did he know
you were the man
who'd make me want
to love again.

I know

I felt the way, you held my hand
I know the way, you loved me and then
you helped me see, what I could learn
so many things, and in return
I give you my faith, my hope and belief
I want you to know, you'll always have me
I want to be all, that you'd ever want
but I need to know, that's how it ought -
if it's the same way, and you believe too
that it's our love, that's pulled you through
to where I will be, always waiting for you
God gave me your heart, so I could be free
to love you forever, as much as I pleased
He didn't tell me, how long that would be
or that I would always, want you near me
that I would miss you, my only true love
and that "forever," wouldn't be long enough
He didn't tell me, how much it would be
that I would care, and out of all these
He didn't tell me, I would miss you
every day of my life, and beyond that too
he never told me, how long you could stay
but I know that I love you, in different ways
too many to tell, so many to show
these are the things, that you should know
if I thought I could love you more, I would
but it's too late to say,
it was more than I should.

separated now, by time

separated now, by time and distance
nobody told me, just what that meant
I woke up this morning, meaning to say
that I'll never love you, again "in that way"
but now I am thinking, what I really meant
is that I need to know, when I'll see you again
I want you to know, before it's too late
all of the things that I dream
but I understand, that can't be done
there's too many dreams, that I'd keep
not enough time, to be in your arms
not enough ways, when we are so far
to the extent that I want, to say that you're mine
that again too – will take more time
but for my whole life, and as long as I can
wherever you are, that's all I am
wanting to be, waiting for you
it's all about you and then there's me, too
what was I thinking, when I let you go
I wasn't thinking, I'd love you the most
for much of the time, I have to think hard
but you are the one, who belongs in my heart
you gave me a dream, to last my whole life
now I can't stop, although I am trying
I dream of you here, close in my arms
I close my eyes and find you're not far
and until then, from what I can see
the rest of my life, I want to spend dreaming.

LOVE

has a way

of

healing all wounds.

you are my rock

you are my rock, you are my light
you were the beacon
that shone through the night
I 've loved you so long
and I'd loved you so much
I can never forget
just what your touch
can feel like to me, my body aches
for what it was, that you have taken
the heart from my soul,
the light from my eyes
all wait for you, until you arrive
there's something that left
the day you went home
all I want now, is that which I know
the food for my soul
and water for thirst
all that I need, you brought me first
the first to ever capture my heart
my body and soul, all of the parts
that belonged to me, now went to find
what you have done, to give them new life
for all that I wanted and never knew
all I know now, it was something to do
with the way that you looked – and then when you smiled
I couldn't look back, for such a long while
then I found out, you've already been
you'd captured my heart and hold it within.

you couldn't know

you couldn't know, what you mean to me
just like the root, under the tree
the part that gives strength
and holds it as one
just like the way, you brought me love
you couldn't know, just what you did
you found my heart - hiding within
through all of those days, hiding its soul
you found a way, to make me whole
it looks for you now
since you have found
a way to teach love, you found somehow
the key to my everything
that I want
the what-else-could I need, that I have not got
it wasn't enough, to live as I did
hiding my soul and keeping within
within its own walls, without the love I could give
you taught me to dance,
and then how to live
I 've never felt like this before, but I do now
you gave to me, the greatest gift of them all
the gift of your love
and all of your being
you saved my own soul, and I began living.

IF

I could have held you

I would have never let you go

AFTER

After his wife passed away, he didn't become bitter. He just shut down.

He closed himself off to the world around him, expecting no sympathy and offering no excuses.

Needing to protect himself from more grief, he tried to forget the agony she had endured. They had married in Las Vegas, after a whirlwind courtship. He was ten years older than her, and fully expected he would be the first. Now she had left him behind.

His last role had been to hand her the medications she needed to try and right all the things gone wrong. When that did not work, his job had been to assist her in getting comfortable enough in her bed, to be able to doze in between morphine top-ups.

Thankfully, these were now administered intravenously. She needed only to press the red button for instant relief. He realized she was nearing the end of her journey when she had to ask him to push the button for her. In her last moments, he would know by her faint moan, that it was time. When she had been able to open her eyes, she would blink. In fact, she had once tried to wink at him.

He didn't understand the real strength that she had been, until the morning she slipped away into the next world. Before doing so, she asked for his forgiveness for her failure to live up to all she had promised him.

He woke up with a start. Shaking his head, he resolved that today, he would celebrate that this had been only a nightmare. Today, he would hold his angry retorts and make peace with his wife. He suddenly realized she was not the enemy and had never been.

To his wife, this was the miracle she had prayed for. In return, she was more than ready to leave behind memories of bitter arguments and take on the challenge of creating a new foundation. She made plans to carry out her vow that each day would be a "new beginning."

The journey facing them might be long, but the first step had been taken.

I want to hold you

I want to hold you
and never let go
there's so many things, we could share
I thought it was meant
that we be alone
then I could show you, just where
it was, that you came - into my life
I had hoped you could stay
and that you and I
could be together, alone at last
until we are done learning to ask...

I tried to find, where your heart lives
but what I found
is that your heart keeps giving
I intended to say
I could live all alone
but all I can think now
is, I found my home
a place to lie with you and see
whatever life, and our love should be
I know what I feel, and I feel how you
will always be, my world of two.

I tried to find

I tried to find, how love should be
all of the things, I wanted for me
I didn't know, what you could be
how you would know, just what I needed
you lifted me from where I was
to where the sky meets heaven above
so I would feel, just what it's like
a bit of heaven, in my sight
you held my hand and helped me stand
I didn't think you'd understand
but God sent you to me, to share your gift
so you showed me how, and you just lifted
all of my soul, and all of my being
up to where a new beginning
can teach me how to laugh again
you lifted my soul from where it's been
although sometimes I couldn't see
I knew that you were there for me
you didn't have to say just where
I just knew, that you'd always be there
and if you were sent, to be my best friend
we'll both share a love that
is without end.

if there is

if there is any love and joy
I can bring
into your life, and if there's anything
that I can give right back to you
it's the same thing for me, that you do
if we could watch, the sunrise together
that might help me to say
that my love for you, goes on and on
tomorrow and yesterday
if we could have seen the moon last night
I would tell you, what you want to hear
but all I can do, as far as I know
is wait for the moment you're near
if your heart could hear mine
it'd hear the sound
the whispers of love, that I've found
and if you stop coming
to me, in my dreams
perhaps then, I can get back to sleep
when to dream together
is all that I need
I just want to know, if you too believe.

the

things you did

stole my heart

it keeps my heart

it keeps my heart, so it can't go
it only needs, and wants to know
more about you, and what makes you need
how to become, all that you keep
I shouldn't pretend, how it "should be"
I already know, that I want you for me
if I'd only known, that you took my heart
I'd have asked for it back, that was the part
now it tells me, it's found a new home
that's made it so happy, all on its own
it needs no more, it wants no less
than to bring you back here
so that, it can rest
it makes no sense, it has its own life
it only listens, to the love that's inside
inside of me, is something I know
I've never felt, and it won't let go
there will never be, another like you
who makes me feel
and love, as I do
with the rest of my love, that runs away too
I never felt love like this, before you.

just what I feel

just what I feel and how I love
I want you to know
that you are thought of
everywhere and everything
this love that I have, seems to bring
more to me, than I could ask
you sent me love, I've never had
hoping next time, that I awake
you'll be by my side, whatever it takes
for me, to bring you back to me
even if I, have only my dreams
the way that you left, before you were gone
I can't forget, my dream lives on
it keeps me forever a prisoner – to
be all that I am, I know I need you
what was it, you said to me then
I wanted to hold, in my heart again
it encircles my hand, and holds me still
all of my love, against my will
captured by you, no longer free
until you return and come back to me.

it makes no sense

it makes no sense
it has a life
it doesn't listen
to what is inside
it keeps my heart
it won't let go
it only needs, and wants to know
more about you
and what makes you need
how to become
all that you keep
I shouldn't pretend
how it "should be"
I already know
that I want you for me
it hunts me down
and sits on my chest
it just won't stop, until it's at rest
with the rest of my love, that runs away too
I just need to know
if you feel it, too.

for every soul

there is a place

in the palm of God's hand

if you want more

if you want more
than what I can do
I'd like you to tell me
so we can choose
whatever it is, your heart could want
whatever it is, that you've not got
there's something else, I wanted to say
but I can't remember the words
it was something more, I wanted for you
so that you would never be hurt
how can it be, that I love you so much
it was only one time, that you somehow touched
my heart in a way, that no one but you
has ever known or been be able to do
and how did you know, just how to touch
my heart to yours, so there would be love
if you need anything, I want to be there
if you want anyone, I'd like to be where
all that I know, is something you've done
makes me believe, that I am the one
that you should run to, whenever you need
the one who wants you
whatever you keep.

how did you know

how did you know
how to kidnap my heart
I'm finding out now
you've taken a part
the part of me now, that lives for two
all of my life, spent waiting for you
what have you done, since you came to me
there wasn't anything that I could see
but I have no doubt, you took my whole heart
now it wants to go home, and never part
I see you, I feel you
I want you for me
I need you, I want to
until I am free
when spirits are joined, and want to be one
they always know, when they're in love
they can't always tell, right from the start
but only much later
if they listen to hearts
if you should want more, than only me
just tell me now
so I can be free.

I knew you were special

I knew you were special
right from the start
but you should have told me
that you'd steal my heart
it doesn't matter, what you bring to me
you've already brought, more than I need
I cannot hold you, any tighter than this
I should not want you, more than a little
the way that I feel, when we're alone
the knowledge that two hearts, know when they're home
as we grew together, we found a love
that carries on, even after we're gone
I wouldn't know about love, and all that
and I'd never know about holding back
if you told me you loved me, and I believed
that you were sure
I was all, that you need
so many times, when you're in love
so many things, we haven't done
so many words, I didn't say
I just need to know
that I will see you again

I close my eyes

I close my eyes
to bring you inside
me, all the way to the end
you couldn't see
that I would need
you to be more to me, than just friend
I may have watched you, where you sat
I wanted you and I remember that
so when you first, sat down by my side
you took my heart, quite by surprise
you shared your pain, and after that
you showed me a heart, that won't be back
I took it from you, to bring it home
I never want you, to be alone
I'd like to hold you, and keep all your pain
I never want you, to be hurt again
I want to know, who you are now
I think we belong, that it's meant somehow
if I can keep you safe with me
I want you to know, that you'll never need
you won't ever need, to be alone
I give you my heart, and my heart is your home
you're safe inside, my world of two
there's only me, and there's only you
I want you to feel, and I want to show
I want to tell you, so you will know
that what you should, have been today
is told that you're loved, in every way.

a lifetime partner

He had left her to watch for his return. Although a sudden request, her eyes had not wandered from the spot she had last seen him disappear.

Her body was motionless while she waited, not knowing the exact moment he would walk back into her life.

But she was determined to wait, for however long it took.

As the hours went by, she began recalling many precious moments they had shared in the past – as friend, companion and lifetime partner.

No one else would she rather be with, no one else she could trust with her life.

Sometimes no words were needed.

On other occasions, one word was enough to communicate a need.

Kindred spirits perhaps?...

but more likely, a dog ...

Dogs know the secret to maintaining a relationship that produces complete and utter devotion, a bond that is severed only by death.

Dogs instinctively follow ten rules to relationship survival:

1. listen carefully
1. give undivided attention to your partner
2. treat each request, no matter how trivial – as the most important thing
3. respond quickly
4. acknowledge the uniqueness of your partnership
5. express gratitude often
6. have eyes for no one else
7. forgive mistakes
8. if there is misunderstanding, correct it immediately
9. obey without question, as long as he feeds you

I want to

I want to hold you, love you
and keep you forever, until the day that I die
and even then, the memories you loved me
will go on and have their own life
if you don't understand
then take my hand
I don't ever, want to let go
I'll take you to places
you've never been
and that we'll just never know
until we're together, able to come
to be the ones to share all our love
the joy that I feel, is something so real
I just know it won't come again
until and unless, and not instead
since we've become more than just friends
I've told him I love him
I know it was magic
and I don't want anything more
I'll love him forever
I'll love him tomorrow
with a love, I've not known before.

I need you

I need you
when no one's around
I want you
all to myself
I cannot dream
without you here
unless I am homeward bound
my heart leads the way
and I must follow
wherever it chooses to go
it leads me to you
it cannot be stopped
and somehow
it seems to know
yours arms would be the one sweet thing
that I will never forget -
but you should have said
you'd come back for me
the day before
you left.

from the words

from the words you couldn't say
your spirit found a way
to open my heart, to feel everything
that I could possibly want
you fed my soul
and gave me more things
to warm me, than I had thought
you taught me to feel
and to seek what I want
now all I want, are my dreams
how dreams and love become the same
I'm not really sure, of their name
but just in case
you can't love me back
I want you to know
how I only want you
to keep the memory
of things that we knew
two hearts that meet
and are joined forever
two souls that seek
alone or together
sometimes it is God
who can only bring love
sometimes it's his plan, that love's not enough.

how don't you know

how don't you know
what you did to me
the power of love
that brought me such peace
how can't you feel
all that you are
perhaps it's because
you're just too far
I close my eyes
not sure of my place
so many ways, I remember your face
eyes, that seemed to want to speak
the hug I thought, was just for me
the things I never knew, that I
would come to love, but for the time
time always working
to keep us apart
but not the way, that my own heart
wants to be there
for every day
to be part of your life,
for yesterday
today and tomorrow, the rest of my life
I'll only love you
for as long as you like.

you will always

you will always ever be
the only man I need
and if my love
means that I wait
then that shall also be
you are the one
who made me forget
how I knew love, and that it had left
I might have said
something else to you
if I'd only known
what I should do
to see your face, and hold your hand
you'd have to know love
to understand
the time we have left, is not enough
if it's to be spent
with the one that I love
but I won't ask
if you need me, again
if you would only
let my love in.

Meeting Men Elsewhere

One of the first things a woman is first attracted to, is the sound of a man's voice.

A deep resonant voice that sounds authoritative can be a powerful aphrodisiac for the woman who likes being told what to do.

A woman who feels threatened by that, is more likely to fall for a man with a higher-pitched, but softer tone.

She is apt to value qualities of kindness, and a gentler spirit.

Another attribute that is admired is the look in a man's eyes. Most women say that they know at first glance if there will be a connection later.

Eyes cold as ice, are attractive for the woman who likes to dance with wolves, although they will most likely never settle down.

Eyes that smile often reflect a patient personality. Patience is a virtue when women like to feel that explanations for their behaviour are being heard.

While some women's behaviour may appear to be irrational to men, it is always hoped that explanations that are listened to, are better understood.

Which is why, Katrina was most struck by the fact that she met her future husband in the kitchen. She had arrived unwillingly for a family dinner, feeling rushed because she had left the work she had not yet finished, piled up on her computer desk.

Then she saw him in the kitchen, making tea for guests. Surprised and delighted to find a man who knew his way around the kitchen, she decided she might be staying for dinner, after all.

She had rehearsed so many explanations to justify an early departure that was one of the reasons she had not finished her project report.

Katrina surveyed the ripple of his muscles as much as she could, through the thin white t-shirt he was wearing, and decided that getting to know him could have its advantages. So much for the eyes and voice, that she could explore later.

In fact, she suddenly felt rather hungry.

what if

what if our love, is not meant to be
or if you weren't, even sent to me
what if I, wanted you to be mine
how could I then, forget you in time
you came to me, full of loving and trust
what if, my love for you's not enough
"enough" is what I need for me
enough is what I think, that you'll be
I suppose I could say, that you've already given
more than enough, that I now keep within
all of the love, that you brought to me
so now I have more than enough, to keep
all of my memories of you, that are mine
these are the things, that I'll have for life
I close my eyes, and you come back
you bring me your smile, and I hear you laugh
it fills me up, more than you know
I cannot sleep, since you had to go
so I wait for you now, I need to believe
that you are going, to come back for me
but what if, I didn't tell you my dreams
you could've said, love isn't all that it seems.

how should I

how should I know
or ever expect
that you are the one, who is coming back
what if you'd never, shown me your heart
I'd never have found it, so hard to part
perhaps it was, the way that you looked
when you held my hand, but then you took
both of my hands, and all of my heart
so each time I think, that it's too hard
I remember you saying, now trust in me
rejoice in the way, that I make you feel
remember our love, it's for all time
one day I'll be back, and you will be mine
you gave me a smile, to last my whole life
now I want you, to be part of my nights
you brought me the sun, to light up my days
you bought me flowers, to plant every day
you came to my side, and in my dreams
so that I would know, I can believe
wherever I am, I'll know your touch
and I'll remember, the kind of love
that follows me, it catches me
it needs me, to survive
a love like ours, was always meant
to last us the rest of our lives.

it's the way

it's the way that you kissed me
and held me tight
that makes me dream, all through my nights
there was love in your eyes, then your caring smile
that made me believe, in our love and while
my heart said "hold on", and then said "let go"
what do you do, now that you know
when you find true love, you must give it a chance
believe in the way, that we're meant to dance
sometimes it will rain, then sometimes it will
be more like a storm that comes, but until
the sun cannot shine, and the moon will not glow
my love for you, just keeps on growing
it has its own life, with its own will
all I know, is that I love you – still
let me enjoy the feelings you bring
let me live now, that you've given me wings
the wings that you brought, take me up higher
they bring me to you, and that is where I
needed someone, to be my white knight
you came to me, and now I just might
have all that I need, or ever desire
except for the way, that you brought a fire
a heat that begins, and grows in me
that cannot be stopped, until we are free
to fly together, above all the clouds
and if you're not sure, let me show you how.

One Night before the Big Ceremony

It had all been arranged. She was to meet her chosen mate tonight.

Her parents had prepared her not to expect too much.

His village name was "Wolf", and he was a ruthless hunter. Although his family rarely went hungry, he did not like to share. She had also heard he was rather vain and known to be cruel, on occasion.

Perhaps his appearance she could excuse, but not a partner who would crush her spirit. She felt the instant that he came into sight, that this was not her soulmate. He gave her a brief hug, the customary first greeting.

They say that a person can recognize the "right" partner, by their smell. If that was so, he was not even close.

He grunted and gestured for her to serve him tea. In turn, she was offended that he failed to acknowledge her during this tradition. He made no conversation to find out more about the woman serving him, already treating her like a possession.

She had been hoping for at least some kind of partnership.

He gestured that he would return tomorrow, apparently pleased by what he saw...After he left, she could not sleep. She had much work to do if she was to plan her escape. It would take careful preparation if she was to get away safely before the Big Ceremony, to take place three days from now. Realizing she would need help, she would have to think carefully about who she could trust.

What had been "good enough" for others, was not her choosing.

While she still could, she was planning on being free to make her own choices.

of all the things

of all the things, I never said
today, tomorrow and looking ahead
I should have told you, I love your smile
I could have told you, that my whole life
I travelled the world, just looking for you
and now you've arrived, what should I do
tell you the way, you make my heart
feels all it feels, and that there's a part
the part of my heart, that lives only for you
a piece of my soul, that I thought knew
my other half, the minute you came
into my life, and then remained
within my heart, where no one can touch
or steal away, all of our love
the love I have, that lives to "be"
all of whatever, you want from me
feelings inside, that just keep on growing
coming from love, that is all knowing
wanting to hear your voice again
hoping to see your face, and then
only when you're closer to me
does my heart understand, how we
were always meant to be as one
they cannot be separated from love
that two hearts should not live alone
unless they know, they are coming home

I have much to tell you, I need to find
so I just hope, that you say you'll be mine
you brought me love, to last my whole life
now all I need, is a little more time.

if anyone asked

if anyone asked, if I'd give you up
how could they, take my only love
I need you to rest, my head on your shoulder
take all the time you need, when you are older

I want you to know, I loved you without
meaning to show you, I had a doubt
but what have you done, that I can't be
alone for a moment
without that need
a need to see you, one more time
a 'want' to make you, only mine

I said I would want, to let you be free
now all I want, is only for me
to be the one, that you desire
to be your partner, for my whole life
for the rest of the time
that I have on earth
I'd like to be, the one that you heard
say how she has, eyes only for you
know that she wants, if you want her too
believe – that you're loved, in such a way
time only counts, if it's today
today is the day, that we become
whatever is meant, when they say there is none
there's none other like you, that I ever met
who makes me dream, and never forget.

far beyond

far beyond, what I'd ever hoped
possibly longer, than I've ever known
bigger and better, than both of us
the product of two hearts
that fell in love
bigger and better. than all before
it leads me to say
that I want more
no one I've ever loved, was like this
it's love that was hiding, and now lives within
you'll never know, what you did for me
unless you remember
how not to be free
it's okay with me, if you can't pretend
it's only me, that can't forget
all of the love, that I have for you
I'll find somewhere, to send it to
I'll just keep the part of you, that I love
the only one I still, want more of
a duty to share, as perfect love could be
I thought what we had, was "just you and me"
the need and the want, bigger than two
all the hope that you brought
I needed that too
knowing that I, could live alone
but understanding now
hearts that need homes.

more to me

more to me, than "just" one man
I'd like to know
just what has happened
but how can I show, what I don't know
how do I explain, love can bring pain
the pain of knowing, there will never be
enough time to love, just you and me
I want to say, that I will be here
in case you need, to find me near
how could one hug, do all those things
with you, they managed to do
what happens now, that I'm not free
to do, what I want to do
I suppose it's okay, just for a while
to never, want to be free
and it was meant, that I understand
what you have, now made me feel
but you should have told me, you'd be the only
one that I'd love, and that you'd leave
behind only pieces, of what I could choose
then I'd spend my whole life, thinking of you
explain what it is, I don't understand
about things that happen, when there's only one man.

I think it went

I think it went, right back to you
though I tried to stop it, before
if only it had stopped, to listen to me
but it said that it wanted, some more
more of what, you showed it could be
much more, than it was before
the "more", it needs, has something to do
with the way, you made me live for
only to hear your voice once again
and listen to how you can laugh
it needs, the way you make it feel
it says, that it needs no map
maps are for when, you don't know the way
and it knew, where it had to go
it's coming to you, it's headed your way
because of the things that I know
you've given new life, it wants to breathe
it wants to know, if you still want me
when I feel you, I need you
and I want you for me
my only friend
is how not to need
I'll always have, what you gave to me
you'll never get it back
now I can live, the rest of my days
remembering how I loved you best
all I can say, if you ask me again
the answer I gave - remains the same.

"it's when I lie awake at night"

and wonder how you are

it's then I see

how much you mean

and wish you weren't so far..."

loving you always

loving you always, I feel that
nowhere else, could I be taken
I wish that sometimes, you'd understand
the way my heart feels, for you - and
if only I knew, just what you need
no one before you, could ever see
why can't I forget, all that we would have
how you were the one, who taught me to laugh
I hope that you know, I won't let go
not ever or never - I'm sure
how I feel, and if only you
could believe, you'd forget about her
my love continues, after you've gone
my feelings of love, go on and on
if you weren't sure, to keep that
feeling, or if I never see you again
let me explain, just one more time
what my heart tells me, it has to find
then let me show you, just what I mean
did I say that, I want you only for me
I'll always keep, the love that I have
I'm wanting only, for you to come back
waiting and hoping
against all those odds
that you're coming back, to bring me your love.

if I let myself

if I let myself dream
your face comes to me
and with it,
along comes your smile
I know that I'm dreaming
but I think all the while
sometimes, dreaming's the only right thing
it takes all my love
and then everything
that makes me feel whole
and then with it, brings
more smiles to the faces, of those who still love
even more to the souls, who are looking above
sometimes I feel, how gentle you are
I know by the way, you've said before
I'll be here if you need me
or anything
tell me, your wants
just give me a 'ring'
and I'll be right there
as soon as I can
so you can get back, to your dreaming again.

what if

what if, I'd never told you
how you make me feel
would that then, make it any less real
you don't have to buy me, expensive gifts
I only want, to re-live my "what if"
what if, I'd never met you at all
then would my heart, still be looking around
what if you'd never, hugged me so tight
then would I still, be wondering how right
how right it would feel, to be held in your arms
how good it would be, to stay near you – or
what if I'd not, been able to say
I love you more, with each passing day
the thought of losing, all that we had
still haunts me today, so I will say that
never again, should I let a day
go by without, my trying to say
all that you mean, and all that you are
it's something I'll never, be too busy for
something about me, wants to be free
to love only you, as much as I please.

when you said you

"weren't perfect"

I thought you knew

that you were

"perfect"

for me...

hearts don't need

hearts don't need people
to understand dreams
nothing is ever, all that it seems
our hearts can hold, all that we want
if we allow them, to see what they ought
you left a mark, I can't erase
imprinting my soul, it brings no pain
it brings me a peace, that I've never known
to know that you loved me, as if I was yours
to hear one more time, if you call my name
then I could tell you, I love you again
I need the days, that you brought the sun
I want your love, to go on and on
I'd like to remember, all that you taught
I know I could learn, if I tried
I want to become, all that you need
so that I can say, you were mine
one's never sure, if this will happen
but somehow, a heart just knows
when it feels wrong, to be apart for too long
I'm not sure, where those feelings go
with all of my feelings, of how I can love
I know that "forever", is just not enough
when you said you weren't perfect
and that I would see
I thought that you knew
you were "perfect" for me.

something about you

there was something about you
that keeps my whole heart
you captured my soul, which makes it so hard
to know that you are
alone over there
I can't be there with you, but that is where
you live your own life, which is different than mine
so now all I want, is a little more time
to show you how much, you mean to me
to send you more notes, so you can feel
all of whatever, you brought to my world
when you first spoke, of your two little girls
the love in your voice, was something that I
would love to be part of, some time in my life
but until then, I can only express
the love that I keep, and I should have said
will live in my heart, long after you
said goodbye to me, yet promising to
return some day
where I still wait
only, for you - no matter how late.

when my love

when my love for you, is all that remains
I know that my life, will not be the same
when summer leaves fall, and it turns to winter
I'll still remember the time, you were here
I won't remember, just what you did
to make me love you, more than a little
I can't recall, just what it was
that changed my feelings, into this love
the love that I carry, I cannot lose
it comes to my mind, whenever it chooses
it keeps me in touch, with my own heart
which somehow today, finds it much harder
not, to be able to run to you freely
waiting for time to pass, so it's nearly
too late to tell you, all that I feel
but another day gone, and I am still needing
only tomorrow, will confirm yesterday
when we had each other, so we could say
look at us now, how much we have loved
but we must now, accept "not enough"
time to love you, tell you all that you mean
or to give back to you, the love you brought to me.

Looking to the Future

She had been sent on a mission by The Wise Ones.

Her task was to find the one man who possessed special powers. The only description provided to her, was that she would know him by the way he could touch her.

Even the brush of his hand, may make her feel faint.

She had also been told to expect feelings that might make her choose the wrong one. Her target was a man who possessed courage, but also a gentle and curious spirit. And she could not afford to make a mistake.

The Wise Ones had also warned her, that real proof would likely come from his power over her.

She shook her head, and wondered if she was really on a mission impossible.

How was she to find him? Perhaps he didn't even exist.

Scanning the crowd briefly, she saw no one special. She thought she would perhaps have to cross the road, but hesitated. What if this was the wrong way?

Her thoughts were interrupted by a strange man appearing out of nowhere.

Nevertheless, there was something familiar about the way he looked.

"May I help you?" he enquired. "You look like you're a bit lost."

She looked up into charcoal eyes that were quietly inquisitive. Should she take flight, or fight? She decided she would respond with a smile and shy tilt of her head.

He carefully guided her across the street, lightly touching her shoulder. She shivered in response. As they stepped in unison, she wanted her search to be over. But he would still have to pass the Test. She had to find the One she could trust with her heart.

I can't deny

I can't deny, the joy that I feel
the knowledge, that lives inside of me
you brought me your heart
so I'd love you, and
now I can't live, without feeling that
some days will be better, than what I have known
when your heart and my heart, have found their new home
you gave me a smile, to last my whole life
now what to do, is for me to find
the first thing I'll look for
is where you are at
then I'll need to know, when you're coming back
to bring me your smile, your love and all that
you promised to bring, when you left me – and
no matter how long, I wait for you now
I just need to know, that you will somehow
enter my heart, like you did before
become one with mine, and then even more
know that you're safe, and that you are home
that you will never, again be alone
and even if, you didn't return
my love for you, is what I have learned.

it doesn't happen

it doesn't happen, 'til I'm missing you
this feeling of love
that goes through and through
and just like the flower
that brightens my day
thoughts of you, sprinkled with my love remain
they shimmer and shine
and then sparkle some more
the way I remember you
makes me feel sure
I know a man, who loves me still
and he is the one, who always will
he won't have to be, any more than he is
for me to know, he's the reason I give
I can't explain, exactly what happened
I only know, when I reach for my pen
to write you a letter, to say how I love
to remind you, there will not be enough
time enough to see, all you do
time to love, my whole life through
but what we can try, to see if we can
is start from today, to love - as I am.

I'll keep you

I'll keep you safe, inside me where I
don't expect that, I'll even try
to forget all you mean, and all that you taught
more love than I've known, or had ever thought
when one heart becomes full, it will then need
the one that it loves, for them to see
all of whatever, their love can bring
but I already know
it can bring everything
I was afraid to tell you, what I was thinking
because it's never happened before
but then I thought, perhaps it's meant
that I learn the meaning of "more"
more than I thought
and more than I've known
my love for you, just keeps on growing
and until you tell me, that we must part
I can't stop singing, the song in my heart
what a gift, you've given to me
the love, that I have been feeling
if they were to tell me, that you will be mine
perhaps only then, I could stop writing.

I can feel

I can feel your spirit, right next to mine
that's where I want it
all of the time
where I can hear, your every breath
right beside me, I can feel it the best
next time I hear, you call out my name
I can tell you
I'm just the same
I feel the same way, that I had felt
when we first met, and I felt myself
leaning towards, all that you were
so I could hear, all of your words
I don't want to miss, the way that you said
if this is love, then you'd understand
but you didn't tell me, all that you knew
and I didn't know, when love is new
that it will always, keep those two hearts
prisoners of what keeps us, in part
the part about love, that's between friends
so it begins, and never ends
if you look for me now, I never left
I'd never leave, what I can't forget.

Cathie and David

Cathie had the kind of peaches and cream complexion that not all men like. But for David, there was something irresistible about her. He would laugh at the way she would blush from the neck up, whenever she was upset.

Cathie had always thought David's handsome good looks came from the fact that his dark hair matched his eyes. She had watched him many times, when they had turned black with anger.

They struck up an unlikely friendship in high school, both being high spirited and fiercely independent. As they neared the end of high school, David gave Cathie a small friendship ring to symbolize their pledge to stay in touch. For reasons neither of them could remember, somehow they lost touch soon after.

As the years went by, Cathie often wondered whether David had made his way to the 'big city' where he had said he always wanted to go. Cathie didn't mind being a 'small-town girl' and eventually met and married Stephen. Stephen reminded her of David a bit, but after two girls were born to them, he decided he needed to "move on" and abruptly left her.

Cathie immediately went back to wearing the friendship ring David had given her. Wearing it now, made her feel like less like the "loser" that Steve had named her.

One Saturday morning at the supermarket, Cathie thought she saw David from behind. It had been twenty years since they had last seen each other, but this man was inspecting the grapes, the same way David used to.

She decided to walk by for a closer look.

"Is that you Cathie?" David called out, His smile was as big as always.

Over coffee, David told Cathie that he was recently divorced also. For some reason, he had decided to drive by that morning on his way back to work.

As they talked, David recognized the ring he had given her. David admitted he had often thought about how his life would have been, if they had stayed in touch. Perhaps that was one of the reasons his marriage didn't work out. David had blamed himself all those years, but seeing Cathie again made him think that perhaps life was unfolding just as it should.

The intervening years had provided them an opportunity to reflect on what was really important and had made them realize they belonged together.

David made a decision not to waste time, but asked Cathie to marry him. Cathie didn't hesitate, except to say it was her dream that he would return some day. She said she should pinch herself first, to check if she was dreaming.

Some months later, they were married on the same boat where they had first held hands. To this date, they remain together. Neither one of them, quite as stubborn as before. All this I know, because I was invited to attend their wedding.

Postscript: David made a decision to move back to the small town where Cathie and he had first met, and as it turns out – fell in love.

This true-life love story proves to us how truth, can be stranger than fiction. When it comes to matters of the heart, often there are miracles that confirm the power of love. You just have to find them.

I don't want to

I don't want to think, any more about you
it seems to me lately, that's all I do
when I get tired, I suppose it will stop
but so far what's happened, is that it has not
nor would I ever, want you to be
without my words, if you ever need
since I'm not there, I want you to know
I've not forgotten, that you had to go
so many things, that you've left to do
so many others, who depend upon you
but that's just the way, you really are
and part of the reason I've loved you, so far
all of your life, spent looking after
all of those people
who bring you laughter
I wanted to bring you, more than your share
so you would know, how much I care
now I can only, wish you the best
and let you know, that I'll never rest
until we are both alone, once again
so I can tell you, we'll always be friends
all of the love, that I've kept for you
is waiting right here, if ever you do
come back to me, to tell me you're home
and I can tell you, I've been waiting so long.

I reach

I reach for the hug in your arms
that was mine
I'd search the whole world
if only to find
the face that I have grown to love
and another way, to tell you I've not
ever felt the same way I do
ever be all, that you made me too
I feel all the love, that you left behind
I want all of your arms
when you were mine
searching the crowd, for what I had thought
I realize now, that what I had – ought
to be in my arms, right beside me
so that our two spirits, could become free
I couldn't see then, what I see now
I didn't feel, all that I've felt
while waiting for you, to come back to me
you were my whole life, and now I need
to tell you the way, I fell in love
you made me feel, more than enough
for two to share, but it's only my heart
that holds all the love, the day that we parted.

no one has

no one has ever, touched me this way
turning my nights, into all days
days that are spent, looking for you
wanting to tell, but only if – too
it's you in my heart, wanting the same
just to hear you, call out my name
I meant to say
how much I love you
I meant to show, so that you knew
there was no time
to show all I felt
there was no "you", so now I can't help
but tell you now
the words that remain
I loved you then
as I do now, each day
I pray that your heart knows, where is its home
but if it's too soon, for it to know
the place where it should
come home to stay
if you run to me, then I will wait.

when I'm not sure

when I'm not sure, what I still feel
the knowledge you care, comes to me
then I remember, the way that you looked
how could I, know then that you took
my only heart, that loves you too
so now I'm alone, living through you
I only need, if you want me to
I only want, what you want to do
I must say it's a change, I didn't expect
now that you've gone and I've been left
the one hug you gave, the sweetest thing
I need to remember, to keep it the same
perhaps you have changed - but I know that I
will always love you, and want you for mine
so I keep the way, you held me then
safe if my heart, so deep within
that no one will ever, take it away
nor could I love, in the same way
that I'll always feel, that's only for you
all of my love, you took that too
so what is left, is only what
I can't forget, when you brought your love.

if you take

if you take another look
at the soul that I keep
the heart that you stole
and that I won't need
it only wants, to be closer to you
it tells me now, that I'll never "do"
it means that it needs, its other half
to be a whole person, to learn how to laugh
it fights to be free, of what I can give
it needs all of you, before it can live
all I need now, is for you to remember
the way that it feels
when we're together
what did you do, to make me this way
how can I live, but for the day
when I will have you, back in my arms
so I can tell you
to bring back my heart
and even if, you don't give it back
that might be why, so far that I can't
ask it or tell it, what it should do
it only knows, that it wants you.

perhaps it isn't

the act of loving

that completes you

so much as the feeling

that you are part of something

meant for two

today

today I rejoice, for all that you bring
whatever it was, it was everything
that changed my life, and gave me a reason
to say that I lived, and loved without season
and if I could hold you
or touch you, and feel you again
then will I know, that you're here to stay
how long must I wait, until you are here
to bring me back, to exactly where
it was, when you had said that day
that you would promise, to try and stay
if I had your arms around me
so I won't forget
all of the things, that we have left -
all words unspoken
with more love to share
or whatever you bring
whenever you're here
you brought me love
in your own special way
I only need wait now
for tomorrow to be here today.

why can't I

why can't I, just tell you "goodbye"
perhaps, it's because my heart says it can't lie
when you brought the sun, the moon and the stars
it knew right then, that it would be far
too far to run, away from your touch
never to feel, and never enough
it wants to know, all that it can
it needs the way, that you're a man
who loves one woman, the only one
who needs your heart, to show you her love
I have more ways, to show you're thought of
I need both hands, to bring you my love
the two that I have, want to be sure
just one won't do, to hold all that's yours
I couldn't carry, all that I give
I give to you, more than I've been
or wanting to give, to anyone else
more than I've ever, been able to tell
only the way, that I love now
is what I know, so that somehow
I need to find, more ways for you
to understand what, my love can do
when I held back, just a little bit more
then I got thinking, what was that for
when all that I feel, belongs to two
and all my love, I should have given to you
but now that you own, all of my parts
I just want to know, when you'll bring back my heart.

I don't want to know

I don't want to know
how perfect, life would be
unless you include me
in all of your dreams
you are the one
who made me believe
and you are the one, whose love I need
while I'll try to protect my heart
if I can
to make sure that this won't happen again
when it lives for you, and wants to be seen
but all that - that, should probably mean
is, it saves its smile - for when you are here
it only wants, the times that you're near
it doesn't listen, to me any more
it seems that it can't, not like before
before I met you, I was doing okay
all on my own, I had my own way
of living alone, not needing you
now it can't live, without knowing "two"
when two hearts know, they are better than one
they won't give up, their key to the sun
because it knows now, it can't be alone
to try to live, all on its own
it's not like before, when it could smile
now it needs you, to make life worthwhile
all that it knows, is that something's changed
it cannot live, in the same old way.

meeting men in the supermarket

He had salt and pepper hair, and would have looked distinguished but for the fact that he was rooting so quickly through the apples.

The ones he didn't like the look of, he would throw to the side in a rough jumble, no doubt bruising the others that lay beneath.

She wondered if he'd been like that all his life, similarly judging women by their appearance – quickly and rudely discarding those that were not pleasing.

One can learn so much about men while observing them in the supermarket.

so alone

so alone in the dark, waiting for more
when all that it wants, is more than before
together is better, and more than enough
once it has found, and fallen in love
it never will be, the same for me
now that it says, it only needs
the way that it feels, whenever you're near
it only smiles, if you are here
it was afraid, to be hurt again
all that I know, is that it can't win
unless it is ready, to love once more
and it knows that it really, cannot be sure
of what lies ahead, until it becomes
a heart that is willing, to let it be loved
when the truth becomes, your only friend
you know that you have, a love without end
when the way I feel, is all that I need
I know that my love's, grown bigger than me
all that I know now, is I can't forget
and for all that, I'll be in your debt
forever and always, needing your love
knowing forever, what's "not enough"
always remembering
how love can be
and how it is you, that makes
me complete.

wandering the earth

wandering the earth, but never sure
until I found out, that you were the cure
for what I seek, to find in my life
that makes my life whole, and my heart smile
what it never knew, not like before
now that I've found you, it needs you more
it cannot be wished, it had never known
when all that you've done, is make my love grow
and although sometimes, it wants to be free
the love that I have, grows bigger than me
so if you would only, leave me your love
perhaps I could find, what's more than enough
it's not what I see, when I look at you
it's all that I feel, when I remember too
the many times, through all my past
I lived, without a love everlasting
but like the tree, that keeps its leaves
my love for you, remains evergreen
fresh as the daisies, you brought to me
they tell me the story, of all that you mean
I can't deny, I've said all of this
I will have to repeat, how I can't forget
something about the way, that you touched
the whole of my heart, felt all your love
something about you, I know that I've missed
now I understand, I've not loved like this

whatever you've done, I'll never know
it was something you did, and now it shows
just how much love, one heart can hold
which we can't be sure of, until we are old.

love is

love is just something, that lives in your heart
you never know when, it's time to part
love is just something, that lives in your mind
it comes when it pleases, then when it finds
that special partner, it needs to run to
it leaves your own heart, so it can be new
love needs to go, where there's no walls
it never says, that it can't fall
but when it does, it cannot break
a love that is true, may sometimes take
a lifetime to find - and more, to go on
moving its target, to the one that it wants
never to "be", is what it can seem
when it runs away, what does that mean
its search won't be over, 'til it's found a home
never again, to live all alone
finding that other spirit to be - all that it ever, wanted to feel
it cannot be captured, it wants to run free
never a prisoner, but a free spirit be
it doesn't listen, it won't obey
it just wants to be, more than today
all of tomorrow and yesterday.

when you stood

when you stood beside me
the way that you smiled
you came so close, I'll never know why
but all that is left, is what I must keep
then you took a place
in my heart that's so deep
it cannot be lost, or even moved
unless you come back
and take it with you
something has changed, and I don't know yet
what I should do, except to forget
but how should I live, without memories
of all the things, that you did for me
you brought me a song, to sing when I want
it told me you loved me, then what I got
is a new way to love, only with you
it opened my heart, and then you came through
from what I can figure then, nothing has changed
except for the way
that you say my name
there's more love in your voice
and more understanding
the feelings I told you, would come
now they've arrived, to change your whole life
and with them, they brought you my love.

just like always

Mike was the typical guy who loved the power of a new sports car.

As he merged onto the highway, he easily passed a few cars.

Whenever he was behind the wheel, it was easy to forget his troubles.

His beloved car had never let him down and he loved feeling the wind in his hair.

But for some reason today, his driving didn't feel the same. Instead of exhilaration from various manoeuvres, Mike felt like he was going the wrong way.

Mike had been introduced to Alysia last night. There was a strange address programmed onto his GPS. Must have only happened after a few drinks.

Mike was known not to keep second dates, so why feel like this?

Last night though, he had had a really good time. It became obvious they shared the same sense of humour as they exchanged stories about annoying co-workers. Plus Mike recalled how expressive her dark eyes had been, turning wide both with anticipation and appreciation. Nodding in agreement, she just seemed to be able to understand even the things, he didn't say.

Daydreaming at the wheel, Mike ended up pulling into her driveway.

As he drove, he must have been following the GPS directions all along.

"You're right on time" Alysia smiled. "I was hoping you'd come."

Mike felt his heart jump at the sight of her, much like he used to feel when driving too quickly. He owed it to himself to find out what was next.

"Want to go for a drive?" he asked, deciding he'd have to trust his instincts. He figured his car wouldn't let him down. Just like always.

if you need

if you need to ask me, what should you bring
if you bring me your heart, that would be everything
that I could ever, want or desire
as long as you tell me, you're not for hire
that what you give me, is what you want
and all that you want, is what you had not
that would be me, to come and find you
to see if our love, would pull us through
and if you then, could meet me halfway
I'd like to be, the first one to say
what I dared hope for, is more than expected
how else can I tell you, I can't forget
stronger than any, I've ever known
and even then, it keeps on growing
it moved me to sing, it taught me to cry
it lives in a bond, between you and I
if you've seen love, you will know when
you can't deny, it's something within
the miracle was
and always will be
the way that your love, fulfilled all my dreams.

if you tell me

if you tell me, that you love me
that would be everything, I need
if I could hold your hand again
to feel your arms around me, then
the peace you brought, would come back to
the way we were, when we were "two"
to hear the sound, of what I thought
could only be, the beat of my heart
I wait again, to see your smile
I have no choice, but to know that I
wait for you, to come back too
you hold the key, to my loving you
a love I know, I can never have
until you become, my other half
long after lights dimmed, you called out my name
and we discovered, when love remains
it wasn't so much, how you looked – I remember
but the way that it felt, when you surrendered
you gave me strength and your beliefs
you shared your wants, and then your needs
and as far, as I could ever tell
you brought your heart to me, as well.

and then comes "forever"

He had no intention of committing to anything more than one night.

She on the other hand, had always pictured herself in the backyard with a swimming pool full of children.

He thought that having coffee had been pleasant. But the only reason he'd said "yes" to dinner, was because he had heard she was a phenomenal cook.

She had decided to set the table with her best china and carefully placed a lit candle in the centre of the table. The pumpkin spice scent would enhance the smell of homebaking that wafted out of her kitchen.

He decided to arrive a few minutes late, just enough to perhaps annoy her. He didn't want her to get the wrong idea about being able to tell him what to do.

She was just putting the last of the dessert eclairs back in the freezer to set the chocolate topping, when the doorbell rang. Checking her hair quickly in the hallway mirror - other than the flush to her cheeks, she gave herself a "pass".

He had to admit dinner was exquisite and their conversation decidedly interesting. The last thing he had wanted, was to have been bored, or still be hungry.

She was congratulating herself on the many choices of wine that she been able to offer with dinner. After the first glass of wine he had really seemed to relax.

He had thoughts now, of how he could invite himself over for a second dinner without appearing to be pursuing a relationship. He knew that there were always strings attached to prolonging a woman's interest.

She was thinking how to ask him if he'd like to have dinner again, when she heard him say "How about my place Friday? You'll see that I can also cook."

He maybe wasn't thinking clearly when he invited her over to his place. His main objective was to establish control in this situation.

She smiled and nodded her agreement. Later as he left, she made a point of lightly tapping his forearm, to let him know that she had enjoyed his company.

He left, thinking that one more dinner wouldn't hurt. Not like it was a real date.

She got ready for bed re-living all the things that were perfect about him. She couldn't shake the feeling that his friendship would grow in importance. And for some reason that night, she started to dream about what happens "after forever".

I hope

I hope you can feel, the love that I bring
since I've met you, I don't know anything
but only the things, I want to say
and only the way, I want you to stay
and of course, why stars are so bright
they're for people in love, to look up at night
for the answers they seek
as to what they are feeling
if you want the moon, I could bring that too
for what you have done
to bring me your love
I can't always explain, how I am feeling
I only know, I can try
to show you why I, only desire
that you feel, what I feel
and know, that I mean
every tune, that I had promised to bring
all that you asked, and with everything
the songs that my heart, is playing for you
those are the ones, I bring to you
for if you had only, left me alone
I wouldn't have known, where is my home.

how can

how can one person, change your whole life
when you find love
it starts to shine
all of the stars, the sky up above
all will look different, when you're in love
it's not the same
when you're alone
if there's two hearts, finding their homes
somehow you just know
when that person stands close
something about the way, you both know
you reach together, at the same time
startling each other, when you both smile
what's more important, is that you just know
what lies ahead, when love is growing
all the excitement, the pleasure and pain
when something's new
it's never the same
if you tell me that you love me
that would be everything I need
if I can't hold your hand again
I'll just go back to my dreaming.

I know a love

I know a love
that is waiting for me
if only you too
could see, what I see
I need you to feel
why "I'm" not enough
it's not enough
to tell you, "I" love
I need your heart
to come and tell mine
that it was also
looking to find
where, it was
that it should stay
and that now, you know today
that place in my heart
is where, it should be
no longer searching
for what, love can mean
I know why I'm living
we've come to the part
I wait now to see if you bring me your heart.

I want to

I want to hold you and keep you
and love you forever
and until I know, you understand "never"
never again, will I love like this
never will I, be able to kiss
unless I remember
how love felt with you
and knowing that
I loved, as I do
I'll never love the same way again
it only happened with you
and then when
whenever, I see the moonlight and stars
I'll only be able, to walk just as far
as I need to go, to be able to see
the place where we went
just you and me
there's nobody else
who could take your place
wherever I go, I look for your face
but there's no one else, who I'd love too
as much as I, have grown to love you.

I want you

I want you to feel
all the love that I have
that's only for you
as only you can -
somehow I knew, you would be different
something about you
was more than just friend
half of a whole, is only just that -
it cannot live, without its other half
until such time, as I see you again
I can only wait, to touch your face
and if touch was all, I needed to do
I could close my eyes
until you are through
but I need to hold you
to be more sure
so I'll have to wait
until you are here
I wait for you now
never again, all alone
my heart found your heart
and then it was home.

when love is a

"New Beginning..."

AGE	LOVE CRITERIA
teens	physical attributes
20's	fun and laughter
30's	romance and excitement
40's	dependability, reliability
50's	consistency, continuity
60's	peace and harmony
70's +	whatever comes your way

if

if I could keep, that love in your eyes
I'd never want to leave
and if I, could keep you
forever with me
I know, what that might mean
if I only see the way, that you were
standing beside me, I'd never worry
about love that's lost, or that slips away
and never returns
though you said it would stay
I'd only want, the memory of
the way that you looked
when you said, you're in love
I search for more ways
to make you see
the things that you
have made me believe
but how did you know, just what to do
when you made me, love you more
now I love you
more than anyone else
that I've ever loved before.

if I lie here

if I lie here too long
I will never sleep
but only remember
the things that I keep
if I could hold you
just one more time
I promise to love you
for the rest of my life
and even if I, can't do that much
I'll just have to wait
until I can touch
the way that you held me
that I remember
I don't have to see you
for me to know - never
never again, will I feel this way
until you are back
in my arms to stay
I can't hold you, any tighter
than you want for me to be
I just wanted, not to need you
as much, as I have been.

safe in my heart

safe in my heart
where you belong
I'll never forget
the memory's so strong
it holds me up
it keeps me together
the memory of you
stays on, forever
thinking of you, and only of what
else could I do
to show you my love
just as the heavens, sent you to me
I want you to know
I can never be free
for it's a power, greater than us
that keeps me still, and powerless
what more can I say
when I'll always remember
the times that we had, when both together
the hands that we held
were not our own
but belonged to two hearts, that had come home.

it's not always

it's not always

that I can tell you that

my love for you, will never end

but you keep coming

back to me, in my dreams

almost as if, you want me to feel

the same love you do

you want to pass on

so that way I'll know - that's what I live on

how can you keep, on coming to me

it's almost as if, I cannot breathe

I know what I feel, and it's almost like

the clouds that must always, be in the sky

the way a bird sings, or a flower must grow

I can't believe, but if I'd only known

the way that my heart, continues to beat

but only when it, knows and can feel your needs

it can't be born

to live all alone

it still wants

to find its way home

somehow it would never, have been alive

if you hadn't come, to make it try

it never thought, that there could be love

until you arrived and then it understood.

The abc's of a healthy relationship:

a	appreciation
b	balance
c	caring
d	devotion
e	equality
f	forgiveness
g	growth
h	humility
i	intelligence
j	joy
k	kindness
l	loyalty
m	meaningful
n	nurturing
o	openness
p	partnership
q	quiet
r	respect
s	strength
t	trust
u	understanding
v	vital
w	well-being
x	xmas
y	you, (over me)
z	zenith (ultimate)

Signs there may be trouble ahead:

a	anger
b	bitterness
c	cruelty
d	disrespect
e	effort (lack of)
f	finicky
g	greed
h	hostility
i	ignorance
j	judgmental
k	keeping grudges
l	loveless
m	manipulative
n	negligent
o	oppressive
p	pride (too much of)
q	quarrelsome
r	rudeness
s	stupidity
t	temperamental
u	unforgiving
v	vexatious
w	wicked
x	x-rated
y	yesterday's regrets
z	(over) zealous

the love I have

the love I have for you
was meant to be for two
so two could share as one
and then they could become
all the hopes and plans they had
all the dreams, they dreamt for them
the love that's built from two
comes only, when I think of you
and then it happens when
I dream of what, we had
though I can't keep, what isn't mine
I look for you, so I can find
the love that you had given me
so I can always dream
the dream of love, I had
was just a need for you, and then
the dream I knew, became my life
but only, if I know there's time
the longer that this takes to do
the more sure I am, that only you
were meant to be, the chosen one
to bring and always, be my love
if anyone asks, I'd have to confess
you were just too special, for me to have left.

if I could

if I could believe
the way you looked at me
I would need no more words
to know what you mean
there'd be no more, that you'd have to speak
you need not tell me, the things that I need
if the love that I feel, would always protect me
and the way that I need, even more
if I keep the memory of when you last held me
that should free me, for evermore
the memories that you have already given to me
they keep and sustain me, so that I won't need
you to be here, to bring me close to your side
the memory not lost, because it's inside
the thought of you, is what keeps me warm
now I don't need, to know that much more
as for me, I will bring
what you left behind
then I would give you
all of what's mine
to give what is left, is only a piece
when it's my heart, that you took from me
so whatever you think, and wherever you are
I hope that you know
that I will love you, that far
if I put my arms out, to keep us together
my love would surround you for all of forever.

did you think

did you think I didn't know
from the moment we met
that we belong together
I've always hoped, that we'd have more time
but I thought I would ask, for forever
I need to bring you, closer to me
so you can understand, what I've seen
it wasn't the way, you said you loved me
it was the way
that you made me dream
I've tried to forget, I don't want to know
I love you much more, than I've ever shown
I can't let you know, that I wait for you
it's something you either can feel, or that you
must know for yourself
in your own heart
if I cannot be there, at least to share
all of the things, I want for you - then
I ask for peace and love
while I wait
if that is all, that I am ever to have.

if I try

if I try and deny, but seek to believe
all that I know, is what's happened to me
the thoughts I have left, are only of you
so I have to ask, what would you do
but what have you done, to make me this way
what does it mean, if for today
I want only you to be near, as I can
to be there with you, but until then
you left behind, a more precious love
you made me feel, how special your touch
something about the way, that you felt
made me aware of a love, that I've held
waiting for someone, now I must know
could only be you, you changed me somehow
what was before, that was 'good enough'
now is so pale, compared to our love
what you have brought to me, in this life
means I can't leave, your love behind
the love that we share, comes only when
I know, that you're going to hold me again
how could I think, I should be living without
when that would be only, living in doubt
I have no choice, but to stay on the path
that sets me free, until God calls me back
so while I can, and if I should be
I'll keep on hoping, you're coming to me
perhaps not today, but whatever it takes
just let me know
how long I must wait.

this book is

dedicated to the memory

of my mother

who never did marry

the love of her life.

"INDEPENDENCE DAY"

The death of my mother marked my emancipation from the memories that bound me to her. They were the kind of memories to be kept hidden from strangers, so that rather than judge you, they might accept you for who you were, or about to become.

With her passing, there was no longer that need for secrecy. I became caretaker of the memories that would no longer have power over me - able to reminisce, select or delete.

The "truth" about my Mom, included the morning my younger sister had discovered her on a spotless white floor, unconscious and in a pool of blood. She had somehow fainted after missing the main artery in her neck with a kitchen knife that was intended to end her misery. After countless tests, she was then sent home by doctors who would never find a cure for the underlying cause of my mother's mental illness.

Childbirth had been followed by electric shock treatments prescribed to relieve severe postpartum depression. Each treatment that followed, only succeeded in increasing her frustration. Not only had they failed to control her melancholy, but she was left alone to cope with her outrage and disappointment.

This was the reason I had chosen a favourite scarf to complete her final outfit. We could still hide the marks on her neck, kept hidden from outsiders for so many years.

Father had already passed on years ago. When I went to empty my mother's room at the nursing home, I discovered various Valentine's and Christmas cards saved by my mother, from someone who had signed them "just me".

I then met Don, an old boyfriend of my mother's who had been looking for "her" ever since his wife had died. I had never met Don before the funeral and since "Don" always had a way of leaving just before I had arrived, I had naturally assumed he was a fantasy created by my mother to ease her loneliness.

At the funeral, my aunts expressed their regret that my mother had not been allowed to marry Don. They speculated that she would have been happier.

Don told me that he had never stopped loving "her" and he had asked her to marry him. But he was not Chinese and of course, her answer was "no", nor would her parents have ever approved. From the day she did not accept his proposal, my mother had lived a life primarily of contradiction and unrealized aspirations. Through the years, she was torn between a sense of duty and her own desire. And she had died, loyal to a tradition that defined who she was, but one that forced her to live with a standard that was unforgiving.

I suddenly understood my mother's animosity when I had divorced my first husband because of our differences. My mother had told me that I "couldn't do that" and had threatened to disown me. Things were never quite the same between us.

Now it was clear to me how she must have loved me. A mother's love can continue even after the certainty of her child's wrongdoing.

Sometimes in death, we achieve all that we set out to do.

My recollections of the past are no longer filled with disappointment and disapproval, but are now interwoven with understanding and compassion.

My own "Independence Day" was a goal long aspired to, but never quite achieved until my mother's passing. Had she "known", I know that she would have been happy.

And I could have told her that I still love her.

EPILOGUE

The way I was told the story, after my parents divorced – it was my father who was finally able to locate "Don" for my mother.

Don's wife had since passed away and he had almost given up finding "her".

AFTER THAT

In the months following their reunion, Don confided that for his whole married life, he had always thought he had married the wrong person. Yet it had been my mother who had married first, letting him know by letter what they had feared would have to happen. In the few brief years that they did spend time together, Don wrote to the nursing home where my mother now lived, asking if they could see her as he did.

Young, vibrant, with a smile that never stopped. Forever beautiful to him, all they had ever seen was a grey-hair woman walking with a cane.

Just a few months after my mother passed away, Don also followed. Faithful to the end, he pursued his dream of being alone with her and now rests in peace.

Then I thought, someone should put their untold story in a book.

I can't forget

I can't forget, nor should I be
the things, that you have made me feel
you brought to me, all of your heart
and in return, I gave you the part
the part of me, that loves all of you
not only for who, but for all that you do
you raised my spirits, you fed my soul
you are the one, who made me feel whole
something about the way, that you love
has made me feel, that there's still so much
more to see, and then to do
what a difference, since having met you
what if we had, never been left alone
I would have never, found you're my home
I'd still be searching, for my other "half"
maybe you too, would still be looking for it
when two pairs of eyes, are better than one
and two hands together, hold all their love
when two hearts can then, only agree
the love that is shared, between you and me
is something so special, so rare that we know
it will not come again, until we're alone.

just one lifetime

just one lifetime, will not be enough
to bring to you, all of my love
what if, you never saw what I see
what if, we never shared love to be
the future holds much more for us both
if you could just tell me, you already know
the peace you brought to me, with your love
although I knew, there would be "not enough"
not enough, compared to the rest
of what love should bring, if we could let
all of my love, come forward to you
so you could feel, all that I do
not enough time, to show you how much
I'll always miss, feeling your touch
I know how patient you are, waiting now
I want you to understand, that it's how
much I love you, when you're not here
is what my heart knows, and already fears
how much you are missed
when you're away
how I wish tomorrow, could be here today.

I can only

I can only forget, for a little while
then all that we had, comes back and I'll
begin to dream, all over again
about what it means to love you, and
then all the pain, the joy and the hurt
comes to me, to live in my heart
for me to feel you again, like before
all that I feel, makes me want more
the love that we had, will always be
something between us, that I'll always need
you were so sure, that I was the one
when you told me that, now I've begun
to dream and hope, and live the way
I've kept my dreams from yesterday
yesterday, was when I was living alone
yet today, I began to live with the hope
that all my dreams about love, can then "be"
but that only happens, when you come to me
the vision I had, of two arms that hold
me only as tight, as they needed to go
to capture my heart, and keep it so still
I could only love you, but if and until
you want to leave, if you set me free
then I'll never love again – see
no one can know, when loves comes to us
all that we feel, is how we've been touched
by something that comes and goes and will be
only so special, as long as one of us dreams.

the grey-haired woman

The grey-haired woman turned in her seat to greet the fiery glow of the morning sun. Her eyes were half closed, but anticipation lit her face.

As it grew brighter, the sun highlighted weather-beaten wrinkles but left a welcome warmth. With each minute, the sun glowed stronger, dominating a calm blue sky.

Her crooked mouth lifted in a slow smile as the heat took her somewhere else. She remembered her dream and slowly nodded her head to the beat of an old tune.

Struggling to sit upright in her stationery wheelchair – for just a moment, she felt her wings again.

FINAL THOUGHTS

Seeing only what is visible to the eye, you may feel sorry for the grey-haired woman in the wheelchair.

But physical limitation, is not as much a handicap as the inability to imagine, or the lack of memories upon which to travel.

I hope this book has allowed you to fly amongst the memories of love that we should all be trying to build as we continue along our journey of life.

May your final destination contain all that you desire, and may you be blessed with the inability to forget.

Tip # 1: the past cannot hurt you, unless you did not learn from it

Tip # 2: if you cannot learn from the past you can expect to repeat the same mistakes again

Tip # 3: painful memories are the reason you know when you are having a good time

Tip # 4: material possessions, are meaningless if you have no one to share them with

Tip # 5: it is in sharing, that we achieve certainty that there is purpose for our lives

Thank you for the opportunity to share

and to remember how not to forget.

what a gift

what a gift you gave, with all of your love
my only wish, not to love you so much
if I could love you a little less, than I do
perhaps only then, should I come to you
with the way that I feel, that fills me up
it taps on my shoulder, to tell me this love
could only come, once in a life
it only lives, when two hearts are trying
to find each other, like they did before
when both of them, knew they want even more
of that kind of love, that keeps you apart
until you exchange for each other's hearts
my heart tells me more, about how we belong
so now all I want, is to hold you so strong
I keep you for me, so no one else can
love you the way, that I know that I am
even if I, were to dream this out loud
I'd never have been able to, somehow
find what you've taught me, what you left behind
a love that's so pure, it can't be only mine
I live with the hope, that you feel how I love
I awoke thinking, how far away you have gone
but I checked with my heart, and you're still with me
trying to say, all the things that I need
more bright the sun, the clouds in the sky
all seem more white, since you and I
were able to share, just one moment in time
when I could still dream, that you would be mine.

Acknowledgements

No book is complete without mentioning its partners.

I'd like to acknowledge my indebtedness to all those who have helped me to dream, with a special note of thanks to Des, for pointing the way.

Throughout the book you will note the appearance of the inukshuk.

In life, we all look for signs to show us the path we should follow. I wish everyone luck in their search to find that which makes them feel complete.

"inukshuk" - one who shows the way, a path marker

" from the seeds of today,

come the flowers of tomorrow " ...

WISHING

YOU

BEAUTY

IN THE

MEMORIES

YOU ARE BUILDING

TODAY

Remembering today, tomorrow and always...

A place to record your own experiences with love –

love / life experiences continued...

other examples to be remembered:

About the Author

The author currently

lives in Mississauga, Ontario

with her husband and three children.

Receiving a diploma from the

Institute of Children's Literature

has opened the door to

pursuing self-expression which can make a difference.

Life is all about loving,

losing,

then learning to love again

discovering also, that

life is best lived

when we choose

that which we love

hoping that somehow

it will love us back

and even if not,

loving

regardless.

A previous book by Gwen Editin entitled

"When you lose the one you love…"

refers to "Ten Golden Rules for Life after Loss"

In focussing on the many emotions that accompany the loss of a loved one

the reader is taken on a journey that looks for answers that lie within.

Life's struggles teach us who we are.

Life's triumphs confirm who we have become.

Her motto

"to think, before you speak

to feel, before you write

to know, before you love"

is free to everyone.

what not to forget...

Physical limitations are a visible handicap
but even more debilitating is the
inability to imagine, or
the lack of memories upon which to travel.

this book was written to help the reader
identify the importance
of building memories as you
continue on your journey of life.

Tip # 1:
The past cannot hurt you, unless you do not learn from it
Tip # 2:
If you cannot learn from past mistakes, you can expect to repeat them
Tip # 3:
Possessions are meaningless if you have no one to share them with
Tip # 4:
It is in sharing, that we achieve certainty there is purpose for our lives

May you reach your final destination blessed with the inability to forget.

always + forever ♡